DIRTY LAUNDRY

by

MARIOS ELLINAS

WITH DANIELLE ELLINAS

For worldwide distribution. Printed in the U.S.A.

ISBN: 978-0-692-18328-1

Dirty Laundry

By Marios Ellinas and Danielle Ellinas

Printed by Createspace

www.mariosellinas.com

maellinas@hotmail.com

Cover photo (front) and cover design by Sergio Barrera

To Tim and Robin d'Albenas,
with gratitude and honor

ACKNOWLEDGMENTS

Heartfelt thanks to:

Katrina Marshall for assistance with writing and formatting

JM Olejarz for editing the manuscript

Sergio Barrera for the cover design and front cover photography

The leaders and congregation of Valley Shore for their constant support

Our parents for their unconditional love and for always having our back

Christos, Caleb, and Chloe for being messy, argumentative, and infinitely strong-willed — yet exceptionally free, powerful, secure, mature, and honoring. You guys are the greatest!

Contents

Introduction   9

Chapter 1: Groundwork   17

Chapter 2: The Great Pretenders   35

Chapter 3: Wrong but Real   53

Chapter 4: A Noble Man   73

Chapter 5: Pure and Powerful   95

Epilogue   109

Introduction

Women are wonderful and powerful…created with boundless potential and the capacity for greatness in every field of endeavor…made to rule. Not beneath Man, not as his sidekick, but as his equal in stature and authority, exercising dominion over all creation.

— *Sexy Laundry*

(Marios)

It all began with a play on words one night, after Danielle brightly commended me for washing, drying, and folding the laundry. Her comment—"it's sexy to me that you did the laundry"—was a spark, the kind of edge I had been seeking for an upcoming talk. Days later, I leaped off that edge, delivering a sermon at our church on the subject of honoring and empowering women. Drawing on my exchange with Danielle, I titled the message "Sexier than Laundry." Over the next few months, I tweaked the title and incorporated aspects of the talk into a manuscript. In November 2017, I published the book *Sexy Laundry*.

A lot has happened in our lives since then due to the book: many copies of *Sexy Laundry* sold worldwide; the title ranked high in one of Amazon's top 100 categories; Danielle and I have been invited to speak on the topic on several platforms; and, most important, many people seem to have taken the book's message to heart. We continue to receive testimonials of how *Sexy Laundry* has positively impacted women's self-image and self-worth, as well as how it has improved marital relationships, particularly when men have heeded the book's exhortations. Moreover, we have been asked often to write more on the subject.

This book is our response to that request. "Our response" points to the fact that Danielle and I worked side by side on this one.

What to expect? When we host friends and family at our home in Old Saybrook, Connecticut, we always like to issue the following friendly disclaimer: "We don't know how to pretend we have the perfect home, marriage, or children. While you are with us, you will experience what we call 'Ellinas real—often raw.' Buckle up."

In the following pages you can expect nothing less. We respect our readers, and value humanity, enough to pull no punches and take no shortcuts. Throughout history, women have been limited, objectified, and generally devalued in male-dominated societies, and that has made for grave problems in households, the marketplace, governments, and every place where men and women co-labor.

Men and women were created by God to share the privilege and responsibility of governing everything else He made in the cosmos. His value system incorporates not just what men and women do for Him but also who they are to Him: His children, who bare His image and have the capacity to operate like Him in this world. The original blueprints for Man's and Woman's characteristics and unique assignments emerged out of God's heart, a heart of love.

After Adam and Eve's fall in the Garden of Eden, a pattern began to emerge wherein Man asserted authority over Woman as her superior. He would lead; she was expected to submissively follow. He would use her for sex and the raising of his offspring; she would acquiesce in order to ensure continued provision for her household and good standing in the world run by men.

With this pattern, we are dealing with issues of social justice, women's rights, and the exploitation and abuse of women—and with realities that have spiritual origins. Simply put, things got off track because humans stopped adhering to our Creator's original plan. And we cannot expect lasting solutions unless we get to the bottom of the matter, that is, the spiritual component. Unfortunately, the deeper we dig, the uglier things can get. But dig we must!

Danielle and I want to be part of the solution. We have faced much of the ugliness caused by the imbalance between the sexes and the lack of honor shown to women on various fronts, such as businesses, ministries, and social life. At times, those fronts have even included our own marriage—yes, much of what we are sharing with you we have learned the hard way. Our perspective is by no means definitive or conclusive, but we believe it counts.

After publishing numerous books on my own—which can be a lonely task—I am very pleased to have Danielle on board for this one. I trust you will benefit from our collaboration.

Real and raw—here goes. Buckle up and enjoy the ride!

(Danielle)

Not so fast, Mr. Sexy Laundry!

Marios and I have been married 22 years, and I can honestly say our marriage gets better and better every year. I have never really understood the phrase "The honeymoon is over," usually said after a couple's first year of marriage. Our 22nd year beats our first year hands down (and, as you'll find out soon, our first 12 years combined)! Mr. Sexy Laundry was not always the laundry-folding babe we all know and love today. As for me? Let's just say I've been and continue to be a work in progress.

For 12 years, we had a functional marriage. We loved the idea of being a couple, tried to make each other happy, but couldn't figure out why we were having so many challenges. At that time, Marios and I would drop everything to do whatever our jobs asked of us, regardless of our plans or responsibilities in our home or with our family. It was as though we had to earn points and find favor in the eyes of our employers. Our identity was found in performance — performing well, all the time.

In my attempt to avoid confrontation, I would sweep my true feelings under the carpet and "keep the peace." This meant never questioning my husband when he let me know he was not going to be home after a full day at the office — he was, after all, being trained for pastoral ministry. I would never ask him to help me with the house or our children, even when I was overwhelmed. He was the man with a calling, while I was learning how to perform the role of "pastor's wife."

I'd often heard pastors' wives complain about how lonely life was in ministry and how difficult it was to uphold the "perfect" standard of being a ministry family. We accepted this way of life as normal, and functioned accordingly. We were wrong to do so. We made huge mistakes. And we both were very much at fault. The truth is, at that time, our true identities as Man and Woman — Ish and Ishshah, in Hebrew — were hidden treasures buried deep inside us, and they would begin to emerge only when we began to be truly honest about our shortcomings and failures. Primarily, our failure to properly value each other as Ish and Ishshah.

Marios and I offer you *Dirty Laundry*, a candid look into the issues that so many individuals, couples, households, and even organizations face, as a result of the faulty foundations and erroneous mindsets they have developed about the true identities of men and (especially) women.

We invite you to take a look into the most extreme, daring, exhilarating adventure we've ever been on, one that is revealing the greatest treasure in our lives: our real, raw, healthy household. Sometimes our family looks pretty, but most of the time we are a bit messy, kind of loud—and amazingly free and full of peace. We invite you to read on and dig deep with us. Will we encounter dirt and mud? Sure—but hang in there, because beneath them lies much treasure.

CHAPTER 1:

GROUNDWORK

"Have you been dabbling in pornography?" There it was. First question, decisive moment. Time froze and the candidate's senses flared. Somewhere in the wall behind him he heard a ticking sound, then the hiss of air coming through the vents. His wife, seated on his left side, turned to face him. He got a whiff of her perfume. Byzance by Rochas. He had given it to her on Valentine's Day. The candidate's eyes remained on the face of the man who had posed the question, yet his peripheral vision registered the expressions of the rest of the committee. Three men's faces. Grave and tense, with forced semi-grins that upheld a semblance of professional courtesy and kindness. After all, this was a ministerial credentials interview within a Christian organization.

*   *   *

(Marios)

Weeds are destructive pests in the world of horticulture. Dishonoring behavior toward women is a destructive act in humanity. Two very different nemeses with one significant similarity.

Character flaws are like weeds of the worst variety. The kind of weeds that have the potential to overtake healthy and productive plants, even trees. Such weeds have two ends: the one everyone sees, the green leafy part that grows up and out, and the end that's completely hidden from view. Weeds are masters at misdirection, because they always get us to focus on the part that comes up out of the ground, instead of the part that is actually generating the entire weed. That end is commonly known as the root.

It goes without saying that sexual misconduct is terrible, as are all other types of demeaning and offensive behavior toward women. I would like to make the case that these acts, while horrible and damaging and far too common, are not the worst end of the weed. They are the visible end, the one that the media, legislation, the church, and society at large focus on the most. I propose that we dig a bit, that we look below the surface, at the root of the problem.

Danielle and I identify two issues in this chapter: our society's collective misperception of the identity of Woman—Ishshah, according to God's original plan—and the skewed, one-sided, man-favoring misappropriation of the concept of submission.

(Danielle)

In the face of dishonoring behavior, silence and acceptance are a natural and common reaction. But when women and men accept that this reaction is the norm, or the only one available to them, the most powerful alliance on earth — Ish and Ishshah — is undermined. As Genesis 2:18 states:

It is not good that the man should be alone; I will make him a helper fit for him (ESV).

The original translation of "fit for" is "corresponds to," meaning to be equivalent or parallel to.

As we continue in Genesis 2, we read about Adam and Eve partaking of the forbidden fruit, which the serpent said was "good," and the shame they felt after doing so. Often, the story of Adam and Eve is framed in terms of their succumbing to temptation, sinning, and feeling ashamed. The version most of us heard was that Eve ate an apple off the wrong tree, blamed it on the serpent, and then told Adam to eat it, too. He ate it, blamed it on Eve, they both sinned, and they were ashamed.

Shame. This seems to be the moral of the story. Adam and Eve sinned and were covered in shame. The worst way to look at anyone is through eyes of sin. Unfortunately, the church has perpetually seemed more concerned about the sin in people's lives than about their true identity—as Sons of God, created in His image and likeness. (The term "son" in Hebrew is genderless—it means someone in training.)

Prior to Genesis 2, we read about the sixth day of creation when God made Ish and Ishshah in their First Estate. There is so much more in those verses than "On the sixth day, God created man," but you wouldn't know it from how we hear this story told. The word here is actually *mankind*, not *man*.

Beginning in verse 26, God says these things:

Let us make mankind in our image, in our likeness, so that they may rule over.... So God created mankind in his own image, in the image of God he created them; male and female he created them. God blessed them and said to them, "Be fruitful and increase in number; fill the earth and subdue it. Rule over...." God saw all that he had made, and it was very good (Genesis 1:26-28, 31 NIV).

It is clear that Man and Woman were created equal, in their First Estate, to rule. It is also clear that both male and female represent the image of Yahweh (God's name in Hebrew), which is how He sees mankind even today, in spite of the sinful choices they have made.

Genesis 3 and 4 present the consequences of the fall of mankind: being banished from the garden; the tragedy of Cain and Abel; and the turmoil that broke out over the face of the earth. At the end of Chapter 4 and the beginning of Chapter 5, we are introduced to Seth, the third son of Adam and Eve. The very last line of Chapter 4 reads:

At that time people began to call on the name of the Lord (v. 26 NIV).

The birth of Seth marked a time when people began to call on the Lord. Genesis 5 begins by repeating the verses from Genesis 1, which describe God creating mankind, and then gives the account of Adam's family line, making no mention of Cain and Abel. It is as if that part of Adam and Eve's family history was completely forgotten and they began their life anew.

When God created mankind, he made them in the likeness of God. He created them male and female and blessed them. And he named them "Mankind" when they were created. When Adam had lived 130 years, he had a son in his own likeness, in His own image; and he named him Seth (vs. 1–3 NIV).

Adam stepped into something new when he fathered Seth. He appears to be walking in the full identity of His father, and not under the shadow of the sins from his past. This is generally not the story we are familiar with, but it is the truth.

By focusing on the fall of Adam and Eve instead of their redemption, we have come to accept ourselves as sinful human beings, and as mankind divided—women being the weak link. How many times have we sat in church and listened to a preacher say, "After all, Eve started this whole mess..." Enough of that! Through the redemptive work of Jesus—His shed blood; His death on the cross; and especially His resurrection—God sees mankind as Ish and Ishshah in their First Estate. And He waits for mankind to align with that reality and identify with Him as Sons so that they may rule together.

During our early years, Marios and I relied on others to affirm and shape our identity. Quite honestly, if those we looked up to said something was good, we partook of it, no questions asked. Thinking freely, asking questions, or being unavailable to serve—for any reason—were unacceptable, deemed products of rebellion or insubordination. On the other hand, when our superiors said we had fallen short in some way, we were set back and had to perform better, to work harder and earn points to find their favor again. Needless to say, this environment fostered insecurity in us and ignorance of our true identity.

Although we had begun a relationship with Yahweh, we did not understand the depth of His love or the intimate relationship He had made available to us. Our relationship with our spiritual leaders shaped much of our mindset regarding our relationship with our Heavenly Father. We believed His love was conditional, based on performing well and on pleasing those around us, rather than unconditional, based on the fact that we are Sons of God. We gave into fear; our true identities were concealed by a veneer of performance-oriented service and subservience to the will of men.

Meanwhile, our family and ministry looked like a success, and we worked hard to keep up appearances. Weeds kept sprouting and growing all around us, however. Our hearts were getting tangled up to the point that we could not honestly communicate our feelings, even to one another. Only years later would we discover and deal with the roots of the lies and torment that ensnared our hearts and kept us from understanding our value.

(Marios)

God did not create Man and Woman for one to rule over the other, or for them to be unequal. His original plan was that they would rule together. Genesis 1 pronounces, "let us create them and make them in our own image and let them have dominion over everything that is created" (v. 26).

Ish and Ishshah ruled over all creation—as one. The original intent was for them to rule together, never with one dominating the other. Unfortunately, the fall in the garden ushered in a twisted platform of control of men over women. For centuries, the belief systems and practices of organized religion have promoted a set of misdirected behaviors about subservience. Those beliefs must change, because they are at least partly, if not largely, responsible for the dishonorable treatment of women across the world. Opinions such as "men always have the right answers," and cultures where women are mocked or belittled in jokes, perpetuate the dishonor.

As justification for their control, men have consistently used and abused the concept of submission, with the following verse central in their worldview:

Wives, submit to your own husbands.... Husbands, love your wives, just as Christ also loved the church and gave Himself for her (Ephesians 5:22, 25).

A common thread in the submission message is: women are subservient to, under, and, at best, sidekicks to men. Not only is such thinking erroneous but it is also completely contrary to the message of the First Estate and the redemption that is woven throughout Scripture.

Submission is in Scripture, yes. But in what context? With what mindset? Most of all, with what heart?

The spirit behind that controlling form of submission does not mirror the words of Jesus to "love your neighbor as yourself." When the Scripture tells men to love their wives, just as Christ also loved the church, what does that really mean? It means to protect them under the shadow of your wing but also it means to protect them, support them, cherish them — and help them to advance and succeed. That is true empowerment. Jesus empowered his disciples to do greater things than He did. His crucifixion and resurrection brought to mankind not only salvation but empowerment, too.

I believe this is how men are supposed to help the women they love — not to offer lip service about empowerment, but to do whatever they can to help them live a powerful life, facilitating environments in which women can grow, achieve, accomplish, shine. Such scenarios also allow for the possibility of empowered wives outdoing their husbands in their pursuits.

Seldom do I meet a husband who is genuinely comfortable with, gives praise for, and makes room to consistently promote his wife's superior accomplishments. In my experience, men are generally at peace with women's success — as long as men retain an upper hand. Worse yet, husbands often take credit for their wives' accomplishments.

In *Sexy Laundry* we look at the Proverbs 31 Woman, who I dubbed 31W, as the ideal model: a sharp businesswoman who takes initiative, seizes opportunities, and makes the most of them. In short, she is a woman who is powerful and significant in her own right. The Proverbs 31 passage clearly points out that 31W is trusted and supported by her husband; there is not even a hint of insecurity or stolen valor on his part. Consequently, 31M (31W's male counterpart) benefits immensely from his wife's success, obtaining a seat in government among the elders at the gate of the city.

I highlight this not to create pressure for women, but to show what is possible if Woman is encouraged at home to be all that she can be, and if Man wholeheartedly, selflessly honors her.

Viewed in this way, submission is not an act of debasement, but rather one of empowerment. Some may say the Western world does better at honoring women than other areas of the world do. However, I say we all have a long way to go. And it starts with God's Sons in the body of Christ, today. True submission can only be found in the context of equality in the Spirit and the love of Christ.

We must put an end to the recurring scenario in which women line the altars as a result of the pain caused by disrespect and dishonor in their homes and/or professional environments, and the one in which men seek yet another remedy to their chronic addiction to pornography. We must deal with the root issue—the lack of respect for Woman. There is a way for Ish and Ishshah to live harmoniously and to continually strengthen one another, establishing us as powerful entities on the earth and enabling us to rule and reign with Christ—as equals.

In the verse right before "Wives, submit to your own husbands," Paul begins with each of us submitting to one another in the fear of God.

That's a very robust directive. If we are called to submit ourselves one to another in the church, then how much more so in the home?

We are accountable one to another to submit one to another. There are different functions within that submission. We are called to different responsibilities, and we exhibit different personalities that bring the Kingdom of God forth. In all of those differences, value and equality remain.

One more thought regarding the erroneous perception of men being superior:

By the same token, the man was not created because the woman needed him; the woman was created because the man needed her (1 Corinthians 11:9 TPT).

I had a spiritual encounter in a dream, in which I better understood more about Mary, the mother of Jesus. Jesus spoke to Mary from the cross and told her she would be moving in with John. And he commanded John to take Mary into his home. Why? Was it so that John would protect and provide for Mary? Or was it so that the phenomenal, mystical, revelatory Mary could instruct and train John for his upcoming Revelation at Patmos? In my encounter with Mary, she was not meek and mild, not a Mary who submits to everything and keeps her mouth shut. She was fiery and she was powerful. I promise you — that is who she truly is!

So then, I have to insist that in the Lord, neither is woman inferior to man nor is man inferior to woman (1 Corinthians 11:11 TPT).

The strategic relationship of Ish and Ishshah is boundless, and it leads to the fullness of life. Controlling, authoritative, religious, legalistic environments are limiting; they prohibit growth and advancement. Loving, honoring homes, families, and communities enable everyone to move forward and maximize their potential. Within proper environments of love and empowerment, there is ease and fruitfulness with less effort and strain.

In sharing this message, we are pushing against mindsets that have prevailed for centuries. We feel the weight of the matter when we broach the subject locally and across the globe. We sense it in our private conversations and in smaller church group meetings. And the resistance and opposition we sometimes encounter are further proof of the significance and timeliness of our message. Enough is enough. We do not want to be limited; we are pulling up the weeds from the roots. We are confronting the issues head-on. You're in this with us now — don't stop reading!

CHAPTER 2:

THE GREAT PRETENDERS

An insider had warned him about that particular question weeks earlier. "They're not just evaluating your answer regarding pornography. It's your reaction, too — facial expression, fidgeting, the tone of your voice, how long you wait to respond — and mind you, they always ask it differently, and when you least expect it."

The insider had been proven correct. In all his preparations for the question often referred to as "the big one," the candidate had not considered that it might be the interview's opener. But how could it not have been the foremost question? The news had been inundated with stories about a media probe involving the immoral standards of a famous evangelist. Moreover, within the very organization from which the candidate was seeking a ministerial license, there had been three cases of sexual misconduct in the last few months. Guilty pastors had been terminated from their churches. Marriages were in shambles and congregations were confused and angry. As the day of the interview approached, the insider had kept the candidate informed of the most recent developments. "The disciplinary board had another tough case last week. Young guy. Only married for a couple years. He was watching it on the internet. Felt convicted about his sin. Confessed it to a fellow pastor, who then turned him in to headquarters. He had to turn him in, right? Wouldn't you?"

*   *   *

(Danielle)

"Hey, how's it going, Marios?" our colleague asked, shaking my husband's hand and continuing to talk to him without acknowledging my presence. *Oh no you don't*, I thought. I had learned how to navigate such interactions at pastors' gatherings: wait for a break in the small talk and then cut in abruptly.

"Hi, how are you? How is your wife?" I asked, slinging my hand forward. Immediately, he sent a look of shock my way; an uncomfortable attempt to pacify me followed. "Um...hi, yeah...great, thanks," he blurted out, eager to return to questions about church size, offering amounts, and the numerous other things pastors count (that don't really count).

Over time I had learned to be quiet, though I never ceased to make men in these circles a little uncomfortable with my abrupt greetings. It was somewhat entertaining, but mostly disappointing. Sadly, this was our norm.

For years—12, to be exact—Marios and I functioned similarly in most social situations. We were in pastoral ministry, and although we tried to do better, this was our reality. I was the pastor's wife and he was the pastor. I'd learned that appearances were important and silence was paramount.

During my teen years, and as a young woman, I was objectified multiple times, naively believing that the man who was showing affection toward me truly valued me. After some time, and his getting what he really wanted, I'd never see him again.

Being ignored or avoided in ministerial circles was a different dynamic altogether, but once again I was being treated as an object and not as a valuable person—a result of the same root issue: fear of heart-to-heart interaction, due to the learned objectification of women. I was dealing with ministry leaders who were either afraid of interacting with women or had been cautioned about doing so. I'd heard the other side of it so many times: "Don't ever meet with a man alone. Be sure someone else is in the room, or the door is cracked and another person is sitting right outside." This kind of caution is understandable when it's about men and women who are known to struggle with lust or perhaps marital trouble, but the people I was meeting were of reputable character and fruitful ministries. Were we protecting our flocks and one another, or were we giving room to suspicion and paranoia?

Why all the warnings and defensive protocols? Why couldn't brothers and sisters trust each other to interact in purity, freely? Jesus spoke to the Samaritan woman at the well alone, and she'd had five husbands. According to the law, there were so many reasons He shouldn't have talked with her, but He walked with a pure heart and could see her for who she really was. He was able to look beyond her sin and her past in order to minister to her. He was not afraid of her.

Lust is not a matter of circumstance; it is a matter of the heart. If the heart is pure, there is no room for lust to appear or fester in a relationship. The issue in such cases is not lust, but the fear of lust, and that is what must be dealt with.

We should not ignore or avoid the issue, using as excuses our past or our gender — or saying lustful is 'just the way we are'. Men and women discredit God and themselves with this thinking. God did not create mankind to naturally carry lust in their hearts, to be tempted, and to not be able to stop themselves from sinning. On the contrary, God equipped us to overcome temptation; He made a way for all, men and women alike, to walk in purity. That way is not to avoid or ignore the opposite gender. As believers, ministry leaders or not, we are tasked with growing and maturing as men and women.

We will not be able to step into our authority to rule over the earth if we cannot even have an adult conversation with one another by way of honor and value. It won't happen. We're talking about Sonship here. If we can't honor each other, and value each other, treasuring one another with pure hearts, we won't be able to walk in the fullness of who we truly are as men and women.

I am thankful to my husband, my father, my brothers, and a handful of male friends with whom I have built relationships and who genuinely honor me. They do not fear me because of my promiscuous past; they do not feel uncomfortable because I am a woman. They see me for who I am now, and we have each other's best interests in mind. Along with Yahweh's unconditional love, these men have helped empower me to find my value and voice as a woman again.

A male ministry colleague recently asked me about our first 10 years in ministry, those days when my identity was wrapped up in being the pastor's wife instead of being in the intimacy of my Father. I responded candidly, and he thanked me for doing so. I really don't know any way to be except vulnerable. The days of keeping up appearances and fearing men are long gone. Looking pretty and staying silent is no longer the norm for me.

(Marios)

As I describe in *Sexy Laundry*, an unsightly birthmark on half my face destroyed my prospects for any romantic relationships with women throughout my adolescence and young adulthood. On the positive side, however, my painful experience forced me to pursue pure, platonic friendships, through which I began to understand and appreciate women. At a time when other boys were learning the cultural norm of objectifying women, I was learning to value them for their character and worth, qualities that went far beyond physical appearance and sex appeal.

Nonetheless, I was being raised in a culture that often undermined women. I knew Woman was powerful and valuable, yet the environment around me afforded little or no opportunity for me to express my understanding. I kept my findings to myself, feeling pressure to conform to the ways of my peers and society at large.

Unfortunately, after surrendering my life to Christ, marrying Danielle, and starting on our journey in ministry, I discovered that mindsets within the church world were not much better than what I had experienced growing up. Church leaders were, of course, decent and respectful toward women, and they certainly paid lip service to women's value and worth, but the ecclesiastical systems and processes within denominational movements kept women side-lined and limited.

It was expected of me to have Danielle by my side at ministerial events—most of which were male-dominated—however, it was also expected that she would keep a low profile when it came to speaking or taking initiative. Once again, I chose to go with the flow and play along. I had yet to learn how to fully support and value Danielle for who she was from heaven's vantage point.

In those moments where men were awkward and uncomfortable around Danielle, I felt forced to be diplomatic, to smooth things over and keep the peace. I was wrong to do so, and I have long since repented before God and my wife for my mistakes.

As Danielle mentioned, years ago I was being groomed, and our family was being evaluated, for ministry. I was *the man* and *the leader* of the church. Danielle had to submit to me, and we both had to submit to the system—a system that outwardly expressed respect for women, but was by no means empowering them to operate in their fullness. On many occasions we witnessed formal presentations in which a man would be honored for something, and upon his receipt of the award, someone would shout out an awkward afterthought—"Hey, let's get your wife up there with you. C'mon (wife's name), go up to the stage with your husband." Then either the recipient or the presenter would inevitably repeat that tired cliché of "Behind every successful man is a beautiful woman..." We were sick of it. Aren't you? We operated within a system of great pretenders. Unfortunately, we learned how to play that game rather well: look good, act well, and make sure things run smoothly.

Thankfully, things began to change when the Holy Spirit moved powerfully within our church. Danielle and I, along with many members of our congregation, started to recognize our true identity, and we understood where we had gone wrong in conforming to a dysfunctional system. At the same time that God was moving in our midst, Danielle and I received additional confirmation about what were up against through observations we made about our town's community. We began to understand the detrimental impact of superficiality and the value of authenticity. It has made all the difference!

(Danielle)

Moving from a diversely populated, lower-income town to the quaint shoreline town of Old Saybrook was a culture shock, to say the least. I vividly remember the long walk from the elementary school's parking lot to the cafeteria where I would pick my children up. In the beginning I was encouraged by a handful of friendly smiles, and even a few conversations, hopeful that these parents would soon become friends.

With time, however, it became evident that the smiles and small talk did not constitute a door that was open for relationship. Many times, when I recognized a friendly face from the day before and started to say "Hi," that friendly face would either blankly stare at me or quickly turn away as if I was a stranger. I would find myself bewildered, wondering, "Didn't we have such a nice talk yesterday? Didn't I even go home and tell Marios about this great person I met and felt we'd connect with?" Somehow, there was an obstacle to going deeper.

My daily walk to pick up our children quickly turned from hopeful and promising to dreadful. It reminded me of the insecure days of high school.

For a while I was fooled, thinking eventually we would fit into the perfect families of this little town, but over time Marios and I realized that even if we did end up in a friendly interaction with another parent, we should not expect to interact with them in the same friendly way again. Repeatedly, both of us have found ourselves in the grocery store or at a sports game, making an attempt to say hello or strike up conversation, only to be given the cold shoulder or a blank stare as if the person has never seen us before.

As the Holy Spirit began to move, we became enlightened to the pretending, in both the church and our own community. We began to realize that we could not go deeper into our relationships with God if we were pretending. It was dishonest and exhausting, trying to be the perfect pastoral family at church and the perfect parents of perfect children in our community. Actually, it was impossible!

Around this time, the middle school principal called us about an incident involving our middle son, Caleb. He asked us to come immediately to the school for a meeting. Marios and I made a decision, on the way to the school, that no matter what we walked into, we would express love for Caleb rather than anger. The principal informed us of what Caleb had done, which we agreed was inappropriate and deserving of consequences. We were more appalled, however, when the principal assured us that he told Caleb, "That's not the way pastors' kids should behave." Although Caleb had messed up, he did not deserve to be shamed on the grounds that he was the pastor's kid! From that day forward, we made it very clear that we would not stand for our children being put under that kind of pressure, to be perfect pastor's kids. They were kids, and they were going to mess up. No more pretending for the Ellinas family.

(Marios)

We love our community — it is truly the finest town we could have asked to raise our children in. A few years into the scenarios Danielle described above, we recognized that our experiences with others in the town mirrored the experiences that millions of people have had with the church for ages.

Throughout the Christian world, church day is a weekly gathering of "the great pretenders." Within the confines of a worship service or the fellowship afterward, everyone seems to get along and be genuinely interested in relationship. Once Monday rolls in, things change.

Our painful social interactions in town helped us think about the type of church community we did not want to participate in, much less lead. We began to seek, establish, and foster genuine heart-to-heart connections. We understood that we probably would have fewer relationships that way, but at least there would be depth and substance in whatever developed.

To us, our church is a core of 30 to 40 people whom we trust and with whom we have navigated many treacherous and stormy seas. We have grown in love, we have enjoyed our times together, and, above all, we have kept it real.

This does not mean we have always gotten it right; however, therein is the beauty of genuine relationship with and in God. We don't have it all together, but we continue to work through our issues and we passionately, sincerely pursue relationship.

For years now, everyone who joins our church family, and becomes part of our community, has said something like this: "I love this place because you guys are the real deal." They don't mean we are ideal or flawless; they mean we don't try to cover over what is obviously not OK. We work on it, we communicate, and we improve.

This is the spirit that must prevail in our attempt to right the wrongs that have been perpetually committed against women. We have to be honest about our failures, admit our wrongdoings, and change. Any church — any group of Christ followers — that can do that will attract the broken people seeking a life in God in the days ahead. What's more, it will also attract current believers who are no longer interested in pretense and a superficial church life.

CHAPTER 3:

WRONG BUT REAL

The credentialing board had to know, so they framed their inquiry in a way that left no wiggle room. "Are you addicted to pornography?" was too subjective. "Have you ever looked at it?" was beyond the scope of the meeting; the candidate could have committed the transgression before he turned his life over to Christ and was forgiven of all wrongs. "Have you been dabbling...?" was just right – it would settle the issue, granting a green light for a continuation of the interview or a termination of the process, indefinitely.

The candidate was aware that the stakes were high. He'd been warned. The insider, nearing retirement, had been a strong leader and a respected statesman within the organization. In addition to having led numerous congregations as their pastor, the insider had also served as a senior official in the denomination's high command. Along with his peers, he had worked hard to maintain doctrinal beliefs, practices, and high standards of faith and conduct. The insider liked the candidate and wanted to see him succeed; hence his offer of interview tips and general advice. "You're passionate and teachable. I believe you can go far with us...if you can keep from messing up." It had to be uttered – the ever-present condition; the mandatory disclaimer. How could a seasoned leader *affirm an aspiring protégé without mentioning the possibility of utter failure?*

*   *   *

(Marios)

Wrong but real. It's the standard I live my life by. But what other options are there—right but fake? Hasn't that been the norm? Hasn't a certain fakeness—a hypocrisy, even—been the yeast in the dough that millions of Christians have been kneading and baking for centuries?

More times than I care to remember, I have witnessed the following phenomenon. Ministers preach against sin and implore people from the audience to repent. Certain sins are listed and members of the congregation are asked to examine their hearts and to respond accordingly. The list of vices is always the same—drinking, drugs, tobacco, gambling, lying, stealing, disrespecting authority (they always make sure that one is in there), fornication, adultery, pornography... "Repent, repent now!" shouts the preacher, as people begin to leave their seats and make their way down to the front of the building.

I must clarify that I find no wrong with ministers preaching against sin, or with people recognizing their wrongdoing and repenting. I respect that element of our faith. What I am appalled by is hypocrisy.

Honest sinners are less of a problem for God than self-righteous hypocrites are. It would be hard to count how many times I have been around leaders who have, within an hour or so of delivering a "fire and brimstone" sermon, committed sins that I consider far more destructive, often at the very table where they are dining with peers or friends: gossip, jealousy, sarcasm, mocking members of their congregation, politicking, scheming, and so much more. Not to mention being dismissive of and invalidating spouses, daughters, and the general female population of the church.

This kind of gossip and political maneuvering spreads seeds of discord in the body of Christ; the

Word clearly states that God despises "one who sows discord among brethren" (Proverbs 6:19).

Had these ministers' sins of choice been called out, I doubt the altars would have been filled. Why? Because "table-talk sins" are not deemed as destructive as the "altar-call sins" listed above. And here lies the Church's perpetual twofold sin issue:

1. We semantically distinguish between sets of "bad sins" and "not-so-bad sins."

2. We hide behind a false veneer of self-righteousness — for surely we ourselves do not commit the truly bad sins, even when we are guilty of the "lesser" ones.

My heavenly encounters and my maturing in the ways of Yahweh have taught me otherwise: heaven prefers honest sinners over hypocritical do-gooders. I believe that the extent to which we are known and esteemed in heaven depends on how honest we are about ourselves.

Consider the parable Jesus told in Luke 18 "to some who trusted in themselves that they were righteous, and despised others" (v. 9, emphasis mine). Here's the key part:

Two men went up to the temple to pray... The Pharisee... "God, I thank you that I am not like other men – extortioners, unjust, adulterers, or even as this tax collector! I fast twice a week; I give tithes of all that I possess" (vs. 10–12).

I believe there may have been some smirks or knowing looks among the heavenly host or the cloud of witnesses who were tuned into that prayer. Everyone there knew the Pharisee was a hypocrite. He was using the public righteousness he portrayed as a badge of honor. Yet his secret sins rendered his self-proclaimed virtue worthless.

The tax collector had a different demeanor and prayer altogether:

And the tax collector, standing afar off, would not so much as raise his eyes to heaven, but beat his breast, saying, "God, be merciful to me a sinner!" (v. 13).

The tax collector was the kind of person heaven looks upon and says, "We can work with that guy—let's draw him in." The sinner's recognition of his fallen state enabled him to be honest, and his honesty was appreciated. Jesus indicated that through his conclusion:

I tell you, this man went down to his house justified rather than the other; for everyone who exalts himself will be humbled, and he who humbles himself will be exalted (v. 14).

(Danielle)

When our daughter, Chloe, was about four years old, she was standing and admiring herself in the full-length mirror at the top of our stairs, in full view of the dinner guests sitting in our living room. One of the guests said to her, "You're so beautiful, Chloe." She briefly looked away from the mirror and exclaimed, "I know," and quickly returned her gaze to her reflection. I almost responded, "Chloe, don't say that!" as I wondered what my guests must have been thinking about our prideful daughter. Just as I was about to speak, I felt an internal nudge from who I've come to know as Holy Spirit, to affirm her beauty; therefore, I said to her, "That's so awesome that you know you're beautiful, because it's true, you are so beautiful. Next time say, 'thank you.'"

I've realized many times over that our actions as parents have tremendous power to shape the confidence and character of our children. Shame and false humility are taught from a very young age. Parents desire so much for their children to shine, and if the children don't say or do what is considered socially acceptable, they are put to shame.

Once when our children and I were visiting Marios's parents in Cyprus without him, I was exasperated and embarrassed because three-year-old Chloe wouldn't share her new birthday shoes. I kept taking her upstairs, speaking harshly to her, and she kept throwing fits. Nothing was working. Her motto that day was, "It's my party, and I'll cry if I want to, cry if I want to, cry if I want to..." and she did, much to my humiliation. Later that evening, my mother-in-law graciously explained to me that a three-year-old can't be expected to share her new gifts, and that it would take time for her to learn that sharing doesn't mean giving something away forever (which is what most three-year-olds think when they are forced to share; by the way, a simple explanation does wonders in this situation). After that conversation, the Lord spoke to me very clearly, warning me that if we continued to be embarrassed by our children when they were shamelessly truthful—expressing how they feel, making mistakes, and even misbehaving—then they would become ashamed and insecure and would perform their way through life. He assured me that He can work better with an honest "mess" than with someone trying to appear cleaned up. And then He said, "You would cry too if it happened to you!"

I find it interesting that one of the most important lessons to teach a child is that lying is wrong, and yet many parents demand that children lie or put on an act to come across as polite. Many of us have grown into adulthood being shaped that very way. We've learned and eventually believed that there are things we don't do or talk about, namely the "sinful" things, and that if you've ever found yourself thinking about such things, there must be something wrong with you. My parents were unaware of my promiscuous lifestyle as a teenager and young adult, and unfortunately they found out while listening to one of my sermons. We have since had many conversations regarding why. I don't blame them. They really did the very best they could with what they knew. During one of our conversations, my mom told me that her mother, during pregnancy, would do everything she could to hide her belly. My grandmother had nine children, which means she lived ashamed through 81 months of pregnancy. This was between the 1920s and 1940s. Needless to say, my mother was uncomfortable talking about sexuality with me.

Recently, I had a conversation with a group of women who were sharing their experiences as teenage girls. Although their stories were very different, every single one of them expressed that neither of their parents discussed sexuality with them. At best, they said, the discussion took the form of an awkward one-liner. Most of these women had been brought up with some kind of church background, and yet all admitted that their process in developing healthy relationships with boys and men was shrouded in shame to some degree.

Thankfully, today's maternity clothing boasts of the belly, celebrating the beauty of pregnant women. We've come a long way, but many parents are still very uncomfortable talking with their teenagers about sexuality, and many teens want nothing to do with that conversation. When children believe they are bad because they are having a strange thought, or are harshly reprimanded for expressing anger or making a mistake, they eventually hide what is going on inside and stop talking. They grow into insecure teens, and eventually insecure adults, who *perform* instead of *becoming* who God created them to be.

When Marios and I began to be truthful about some of the heart issues we both had, and we afforded our children the freedom to express themselves, it was a difficult time for all of us. Freedom of expression for the entire family is a risky step to take, especially if the man of the house is used to having the predominant voice. Marios and I would constantly evaluate whether it was OK to allow some of the behavior that resulted from this new way of living. For example, during our early days of ministry, our oldest son, Christos, due to a buildup of anger that he had never been allowed to express, would explode and punch holes in the wall. Of course, this is the wrong way to show anger; however, as a good friend encouraged us, "At least he is able to express himself. Many people never learn how to express themselves." Then we realized that we were all learning how to speak up and be honest, and although many times we were wrong in how we did it, God was teaching us that He can work so much better in the reality of a mess than in the pretense of perfection.

(Marios)

As I travel the globe, I am constantly amazed at how humans have harnessed energy, redirected rivers, built phenomenal structures —

all of the amazing accomplishments in places like the U.S., Singapore, Dubai—and yet I submit to you that we could be so much further along if we honored all of us. Because we generally have not honored, or have dishonored, half of us: women.

The dishonor toward women is as detrimental as the "big" sins that get more press time in the pulpit. Sin is sin. Who are we kidding? Ourselves, those around us, our future, and our God—that's who. We are missing out on the future that God wants all of us to co-create, together.

Danielle shares such great stories about our very real journey, which has been replete with moments when we made mistakes. Honestly dealing with the real and the raw has pushed us to get the wrong out, thus making way for what is good.

As I look back, I cannot help but be filled with gratitude. Gratitude for a wife who so fully surrenders to God, and in doing so allows herself and those around her to be free—without shame or condemnation for what hasn't been perfected yet. Danielle leads and lives this way. I value that in her, because it is only by facing our mess that we make way for God's redemption to spark hope into pure life. Danielle's freedom has facilitated tremendous growth for me and many other people.

In keeping with the wrong-but-real theme, I must share a recent incident in our home. Ish in the glorious First Estate? Definitely not!

Right before heading out for yet another series of back-to-back conferences, I had a bad moment with one of our children. My daughter had cranked her air conditioner down to 60 degrees, while concurrently opening her door and windows in the swelter of summer. The Bible says Wisdom mixes her wine. Well, my child mixes her weather. This must be a good sign.

When I found her room in the mix—for the umpteenth time, in spite of my frequent admonitions—I was furious. I decided to do something dramatic to make a statement. I picked up the electrical cord that connected the air conditioner to the plug, intending to yank it hard to show her how upset I was. Lo and behold, anger turned to rage, and I pulled hard on the *wrong* end of the cord, jerking the air conditioner right out of the window.

A part of me was shocked and embarrassed, but deep down I did think, *Wow — wasn't sure I could still do that kind of stuff.* One big problem: my wife, Ishshah. You want to have mama bear come out? Mess with her kids. Then you understand the silent treatment, the *you're in trouble, in the doghouse, or on the couch for the night* lifestyle. There is only one way out of that in our house, and it's called, "Repent!"

For moments like these, the family text-message group works best. The one guilty of transgression writes something like this: "Hi, this is dad. We all know what happened. There will be a meeting tonight after dinner. I will be the keynote speaker."

At that meeting, you don't try to justify your behavior. You don't try to say, "I've told you 14 million times to shut off lights, and ever since you were little I've been telling you not to waste energy." It's not the time for that message. You are in the wrong. Own it. Eat it. If there's reason to talk about the lights being left on or the power being wasted, have a different meeting. In this repentance meeting, I'm only repenting. I'm facing each member of the family and apologizing for how I messed their day up. To the boys: "I'm sorry that I caused such commotion in the house when you had friends over." To Danielle: "I'm sorry that I messed with your daughter. Let me live, and not die, and declare the works of the Lord." To my daughter, with tears in my eyes: "Chloe, I apologize to you and I will make this up to you." Which basically means a huge shopping trip and money being moved from my accounts into hers. In that moment there was no room for excuses—I simply had to apologize.

All of this happened two days before I was leaving, so I had to make it right. The family forgave and blessed me. It is very important to me to be sent out on a trip with the blessing of my family.

In our home, we have established this approach to redeeming situations with each other. It's one that provides the space for being honest with one another. It's raw. It's real. And it allows the bad areas of our lives to show their head — and root — so that we can swiftly move to eradicate them. I am so thankful for the team, Ish and Ishshah, that has allowed us to build this environment to remedy the wrongs and grow together. Our kids participate fully, too.

What if we did not have an environment where messy is OK — where I was not real with my wife and children when I was wrong? Where would the power go? What would the consequences be? What would happen through short- and long-term impacts? What if I did not value their opinions, their feelings, their voices? If I did not value their blessings — what then? What kind of message would that send to my children on how Ishshah and Ish should treat one another and work together?

Then consider the flip side: what fruit comes from a house filled with reciprocal honor, freedom, and everyone's voice having value? Healthy, lovely fruit — the kind that continues growing.

You and I are the ones who can chose to be real or fake.

After all, who can really see into a person's heart and know his hidden impulses except for that person's spirit? (1 Corinthians 2:11 TPT).

If we are not real, we really can't move from wrong to righteous. Why stand in our own way? We must choose real and receive the freedom God gives us to face our impurities. We must deal with them and embrace the life, the future, and the fullness that Christ has made available to us.

CHAPTER 4:

A NOBLE MAN

The candidate knew exactly what his mentor meant. "Messing up" had nothing to do with lack of vision, poor people skills, managerial incompetence, or even doctrinal error. Messing up was completely about moral failure — physical or emotional adultery, fornication, and, the newest vice to plague the movement, internet pornography. Biblically speaking, such sins were forgivable in heaven; however, they seemed unpardonable within that particular religious organization. "You do that stuff and you're finished," the insider warned the candidate months earlier. He took another sip of Coke from his striped straw, narrowed his eyes, and pointed his finger. "Sure, we can offer a restoration process and try to help you save your marriage, but things will never be the same for you. You mess with that stuff, you'll be done!"

* * *

(Marios)

In *Sexy Laundry* I present the woman of Proverbs 31 as Woman operating in First Estate — a woman living out the fullness of her potential, according to God's original design. By all indications, 31W is also a wife and a mother, and seems to thrive at home as much as she does in the marketplace. I attribute part of 31W's success to her husband's attitude and behavior toward her. He "safely trusts her" (Proverbs 31:11), "praises her" (Proverbs 31:28), and gives her space and freedom to shine.

This chapter is devoted to 31W's counterpart: Man, Ish, who is living out the fullness of his First Estate Sonship, especially regarding his perception of and dealings with Ishshah. The virtuous woman of Proverbs 31 is not a specific individual with a name or a story. And we are hard-pressed, due to the general brevity of the biblical record about people's lives, to find a specific hero of our faith who models all the virtues of 31W. In the case of 31M, however, the Bible does present a candidate. It is a man who seems to have dealt with the weeds and their roots. A man who is righteous, who honors, respects, and empowers women. A man who seems comfortable with the greatness of Ishshah. A man who does not always have to be the center of attention and who creates the space for women to have a voice. His name is Boaz, and his story is found in the book of Ruth.

Boaz was Ruth's husband. Their son was Obed, who had a son named Jesse, the father of King David. Thus Boaz and, through marriage, Ruth are of the tribe of Judah, and are in the genealogical line that ultimately leads to Jesus, the Messiah.

I firmly believe that Yahweh was very particular about the genetic pool of Christ's generational line. Those born into or added to the tribe of Judah generally demonstrated inner qualities that set them apart: integrity, nobility, leadership, purity, and other virtues that are squarely rooted in a heart consecrated and dedicated to God.

Yahweh continues to search throughout the earth for such individuals. People who are so saturated in devotion and purity that, no matter how far they advance, what they attain, whom they stand before, or how great a name they build, their hearts pulse with the purest of intentions and their character is always above reproach. Is this even possible? I believe so, and I think Boaz would agree.

I am very encouraged by the progress we are making in various areas of pursuit and advancement within God's Kingdom. In many of the places I minister, I find greater hunger for His ways and more freedom to explore and discover than ever before. I believe there is no limit to what we can accomplish if we continue to engage passionately and keep the weeds from our hearts. I see a future that is potentially very bright for the Sons; however, I also recognize that the effectiveness and longevity of what we build together will depend in large part on how well we engage in relationship with one another, especially as Ish and Ishshah. Several facets of Boaz's life set a high standard for us in this area. Boaz dealt with Ruth magnificently; his example regarding freedom and empowerment in the interaction between men and women is one we should aspire to follow.

The book of Ruth begins with a brief description of the heartbreaking and harsh circumstances surrounding Ruth and Naomi, her mother-in-law. Ruth, a Moabitess, married the son of a Jewish couple, Elimelech and Naomi. The family had moved from Judah and settled in Ruth's homeland of Moab to escape a famine. While in Moab, all three men of Elimelech's household died, leaving Naomi, Ruth, and Naomi's other daughter-in-law, Orpah, widows.

Naomi decided to return to her homeland, Bethlehem, and asked Ruth and Orpah to remain with their people in Moab. Through the course of their conversation, Orpah decided to stay in Moab, while Ruth was determined to accompany Naomi to Judah, saying, "Your people shall be my people, and your God, my God" (Ruth 1:16). What an amazing stance of loyalty and dedication! What a glimpse we are given into Ruth's virtuous heart! So Ruth packed up and moved with Naomi to Bethlehem.

Because of Ruth's unwavering commitment to Naomi, shortly after the women returned to Bethlehem, Naomi took the initiative to connect Ruth to Boaz, the man who was eligible to become Ruth's kinsman redeemer, according to Jewish tradition.

A kinsman redeemer was a relative of a deceased patriarchal figure. He would take on the responsibilities of the man who had died, in order to fulfill the man's obligations before men and God. The kinsman redeemer had the privilege of obtaining all of the man's possessions, to make sure the family was cared for properly. Because women were seen as a possession at that time, when the kinsman redeemer gained the deceased man's property, he would also marry the man's wife.

Naomi knew that Boaz could act as kinsman redeemer, so she coached Ruth on how to position herself before Boaz in order to see whether he would step up and take on the role. (I call it "tactical matchmaking.")

The plan began with Naomi encouraging Ruth to glean in Boaz's fields. The Law of Moses made provision for the poor by instructing landowners to leave some grain behind in the fields for them to gather. So Ruth went to collect grain on Boaz's land.

Then she left, and went and gleaned in the field after the reapers. And she happened to come to the part of the field belonging to Boaz, who was of the family of Elimelech (Ruthe 2:3).

Boaz had been away in town, and upon returning to the fields he "said to the reapers, 'The Lord be with you!' And they answered him, 'The Lord bless you'" (v. 4).

I love how he comes home from a business trip and the first words out of his mouth are a blessing over the people who serve him in his fields. Their response is equally impressive, indicating the type of honorable culture Boaz had established among his employees.

Boaz said to his servant who was in charge of the reapers, "Whose young woman is this?" (v. 5).

His first question about this unknown woman in his fields was "Who does she belong to?" or in other words, "Who is she submitted to?" His inquiry wasn't from a possessive, territorial place or a position of control; he asked because he was a man of integrity.

So the servant who was in charge of the reapers answered and said, "It is the young Moabite woman who came back with Naomi from the country of Moab …she came and has continued from morning until now, though she rested a little in the house" (vs. 6–7).

Boaz was intrigued. He said to Ruth:

"You will listen, my daughter, will you not? Do not go to glean in another field, nor go from here, but stay close by my young women. Let your eyes be on the field which they reap, and go after them. Have I not commanded the young men not to touch you? And when you are thirsty, go to the vessels and drink from what the young men have drawn" (vs. 8–9).

Ruth was deeply touched by Boaz's kindness.

So she fell on her face, bowed down to the ground, and said to him, "Why have I found favor in your eyes, that you should take notice of me, since I am a foreigner?" (v. 10).

Boaz's answer reveals more about the kind of man he was. He already knew some things about Ruth, and he had begun to cultivate respect and admiration for her:

"It has been fully reported to me, all that you have done for your mother-in-law since the death of your husband, and how you have left your father and your mother and the land of your birth, and have come to a people whom you did not know before" (v. 11).

Boaz was a man who valued uprightness and virtue. Next, he pronounced a blessing over Ruth:

"The Lord repay your work, and a full reward be given you by the Lord God of Israel, under whose wings you have come for refuge" (v. 12).

Out of his generosity and largeness of heart, Boaz went beyond what the law required of him in such situations. He made extraordinary arrangements for Ruth's protection and provision:

Boaz commanded his young men, saying, "Let her glean even among the sheaves, and do not reproach her. Also let grain from the bundles fall purposely for her; leave it that she may glean, and do not rebuke her" (vs. 15–16).

From Ruth's perspective as a foreigner, what Boaz did for her was unbelievable. But because

Ruth left her own people to stand by her mother-in-law, Boaz acknowledged her outstanding character. People who are honoring and honorable recognize others who live by the same standard.

One more important thing to note during Boaz's initial meeting with Ruth. Once Boaz acknowledged who Ruth was and what she did for her family, he made a statement by which he intentionally dodged credit as the provider for Ruth's needs. In verse 12 he says, "The Lord repay your work, and a full reward be given you by Lord God of Israel, under whose wings you have come for refuge" — signifying that Yahweh would reward her and that He was her source of sustenance, not Boaz. People of spiritual substance and integrity know to redirect praise or appreciation that comes their way to the Lord, the One who is truly worthy of praise and glory.

Ruth gained much more than she expected to and returned to Naomi loaded up with all kinds of goods from Boaz, as well as his promise for further provision.

I believe that moment was when the wise and perceptive Naomi saw the opportunity for the marital union between Ruth and Boaz. Naomi told Ruth about the concept of the kinsman redeemer and instructed her to appear before Boaz that very night, as he and his men would be winnowing barley at the threshing floor. (As a side note, having grown up in the Near/Middle East, I have some understanding about how Naomi obtained so much information. The intelligence agencies of our world pale in comparison to a Middle Eastern mother-in-law when it comes to knowing things about people.)

Naomi's instructions were very specific:

"Therefore wash yourself and anoint yourself, put on your best garment and go down to the threshing floor; but do not make yourself known to the man until he has finished eating and drinking" (Ruth 3:3).

Naomi's Matchmaking 101 strategy: "Look good, smell good, and do what I tell you."

"Then it shall be, when he lies down, that you shall notice the place where he lies; and you shall go in,

uncover his feet, and lie down; and he will tell you what you should do" (v. 4).

Ruth did exactly what she was told. She went to the threshing floor, waited for Boaz to finish his meal and lie down, and then "came softly, uncovered his feet, and lay down" (v. 7).

When a man was merry with wine, as was undoubtedly Boaz's case that night, he was vulnerable. Ruth's uncovering of his feet was very significant, in that she was standing by him protectively. My friend Ian Clayton teaches that Ruth, as in the case of Abigail, when she intervened at a critical moment in David's life — when David was en route to kill Abigail's husband Nabal for dishonoring him — teaches that Ruth was acting in accordance with her heavenly identity and assignment, which was priest of Yahweh. Socially, Ruth was a woman who came to ask Boaz to marry her as kinsman redeemer; spiritually, Ruth approached Boaz and lay down next to him out of her capacity as priest — mediator, protector, and intercessor.

Now it happened at midnight that the man was startled, and turned himself; and there, a woman was lying at his feet (v. 8).

Ruth's initiative was bold and risky, as it defied societal norms: a woman coming out of the night to approach one inebriated man, where all the men were sleeping.

And he said, "Who are you?" So she answered, "I am Ruth, your maidservant. Take your maidservant under your wing, for you are a close relative" (v. 9).

It is important to note that Ruth did not wait for Boaz to tell her what to do, according to Naomi's instructions. Having stepped into her priestly role, Ruth went off Naomi's script and took initiative. She was a woman of God, she had authority, and she spoke with confidence: "Take me under your wing, I am your relative."

I admire Ruth for finding her voice and speaking forth. She knew who she was and what she wanted. Moreover, Ruth had found in Boaz, even through her brief interaction with him, a man who would not just meet her immediate need out of mercy but also empower her to be the woman she was always meant to be. Ruth and Boaz were undoubtedly aware that heaven was tapping them for something greater than themselves, and all they had to do was obey and follow God's way. Neither Ruth nor Boaz knew that their grandson would be King David, who ruled so brilliantly that his legacy has endured throughout all generations. Ruth didn't know that the one who would serve her as kinsman redeemer would also empower her to become all that she was destined to be—ultimately part of the lineage of Christ, the Messiah, the kinsman redeemer of the world.

I wonder how many of us are marked for greatness beyond even our greatest expectations, if only we would take one more step to unlock that destiny.

Boaz's response to Ruth was remarkable, and I find in it a noble and excellent standard that all men may learn from. He agreed to pursue his right as kinsman redeemer, as long as another man who was more eligible turned down the offer (once again, Boaz showing integrity):

"And now, my daughter, do not fear. I will do for you all that you request, for all the people of my town know that you are a virtuous woman. Now it is true that I am a close relative; however, there is a relative closer than I. Stay this night, and in the morning it shall be that if he will perform the duty of a close relative for you — good; let him do it. But if he does not want to perform the duty for you, then I will perform the duty for you, as the Lord lives! Lie down until morning" (vs. 11–13).

Note that Boaz told Ruth to stay and lie down by him until morning. Then he gave her a directive:

"Do not let it be known that the woman came to the threshing floor" (v. 14).

Boaz demonstrates two outstanding qualities in verses 13 and 14: purity and discretion. He is pure enough to feel comfortable with a single woman lying next to him — one who has just asked him to marry her! If there had been sexual impurity in Boaz, he might have been ashamed or fearful to tell Ruth to stay. And even if she did stay, he might have laid awake all night with any number of fantasies, which according to Jesus' teachings would be just as bad as committing the act (Matthew 5:28).

Moreover, Boaz uses discretion in recognizing that if word gets out that a woman was at the threshing floor, his reputation could be affected negatively, disrupting the whole process. Therefore, he tells Ruth to keep the matter between them.

I believe men are in a position to walk in purity and discretion, in a way that goes beyond the stern religious exhortation to "avoid the appearance of evil." I believe it is possible for us to stand as men who respect women enough to offer them help and shelter, while assuring them that nothing improper will happen.

Purity and discretion must go hand in hand if we are to model the proper way for Ish and Ishshah to interact. We have to be positioned securely within the nature and government of Yahweh, honoring His ways, and we must demonstrate wholesome, good, upright behavior. Just because our hearts and motives are pure does not qualify us to engage with other men's daughters or wives without boundaries and proper order.

Purity and discretion must be combined if we are to properly position ourselves as brothers and sisters walking together in unity, demonstrating something that provokes the world to admire and follow our example.

When pure intent and good protocol work together in tandem, I strongly believe the bar will be raised high, and our conduct will transmit a much-needed message between men and women in our society: "I am safe. You are safe. We are safe."

Boaz walked firmly with honor and integrity, to the point that he created an environment for Ruth to be safe, to expand and move, and to be bold.

All Ruth knew at the time was that she needed to stay with Naomi, do what she said, and go see Boaz. In his field she found comfort, assurance, and empowerment. Boaz discovered in Ruth someone he could love, protect, empower, live with, and together build legacy with.

I find in their lives treasures worth pursuing — something that really works. Here we see the appearance of good, the righteous way, roots grown in the soil of purity and discernment. These lives come from an angle that is purely Kingdom. Tap into this, I invite you. I promise we will find ourselves in right relations where both Ish and Ishshah flourish, where we augment one another, and where we are established to govern as God powerfully designed.

(Danielle)

It was a group of women in the church we've been leading since 2005 who introduced us to the reality of a Kingdom that values men and women alike. These women met for prophetic intercession, a term neither Marios nor I was familiar with. We found ourselves curious. Marios was the first of us to visit the prayer meeting in our sanctuary, and found himself among a group of powerful women who prayed and prophesied with great faith. During my first meeting, I remember being struck by the fact that they were not at all intimidated or impressed by the pastor, as they freely prayed and prophesied with authority over *both* of us. Shortly after that initial meeting, through many tears, I confided in one of these women that we (the pastor and his wife) were struggling in some areas, and to my complete surprise she did not seem to be the least bit concerned. She just looked at me through eyes of love and said, "Oh, that's no problem."

In the days to follow, Marios and I would dig deep to extract the roots of fear and religious bondage. Upon our decision to step into our identities as Ish and Ishshah, I was learning to lift up my voice. At the same time, Marios was learning to lay his down.

The account of Ruth describes Boaz as a master facilitator, who created an environment for his servants and his family to safely thrive. He evaluated the circumstances around him through a pure heart. The freedom that our family has walked in is, in large part, due to Marios being a great facilitator. He, like Boaz, demonstrates purity and discretion. He created an environment for our marriage to heal.

Marios has always had a largeness of heart toward our family and those around him. One of my favorite things about him is that he genuinely desires for others to succeed. Although it was difficult for him to hear some things I had to say back then, he saw me with unconditional love (purity) and heard what I had to say with an open mind (discretion). Ultimately, he knew the only way he could walk in the fullness of 31M was by supporting me to become 31W.

It is our responsibility as men and women to stand up as Ish and Ishshah, not only so that others can thrive but also so that the generations that follow can be fruitful. Boaz and Ruth built legacy by facilitating environments for those around them to flourish. The way in which they communicated in the fullness of Ish and Ishshah before their union, and as husband and wife afterward, set up and blessed the generations that would come forth.

CHAPTER 5:

PURE AND POWERFUL

"Oh, and your wife — they won't ask her much, but they'll be watching her, too," the insider explained. The men would pose their questions to the candidate, and he would answer them. The candidate's wife was to remain poised and calm, hands resting on her lap, torso upright. This was serious business, especially if a certain question elicited a certain confession.

The candidate had responded to the insider's warnings by simply nodding, yet he could hardly suppress the questions within. Why wasn't the fear of failure, and the potential shipwreck of professional and family life, strong enough to prevent people's moral failures? Was there a force stronger than fear that could procure better results?

*   *   *

(Marios)

I am convinced that fear is not nearly as good of a motivator as reward is. I prefer to focus on the benefits of uprightness, rather than the consequences of a corrupt lifestyle. In areas of responsibility where I have authority to establish my own system of rule, I emphasize the positive and never focus on the negative. Unfortunately, the governmental systems of various religious organizations I have been involved with operate in the opposite way. Especially as it pertains to the sin of lust. The narrative presented here, involving the candidate and his interview process, focuses on a particular organization's near-fixation with the issue of pornography. I have experienced the stance of organizations as such to be similar regarding all sexual and moral sins. Fear-based and limited in procuring good results.

For us pastors, sexual wrongdoing in the form of fornication, adultery, or entanglement with pornography was the ever-present dark cloud that was looming in the not-so-distant horizon. Just one breeze of the wrong kind, due to a failure to adhere to the "rules of engagement" with fellow ministers or parishioners, and we could find ourselves in an epic storm of moral dilemma and, potentially, utter failure.

Danielle and I have sat through plenty of meetings in which the leaders the event or project told us to "avoid the appearance of evil" and "fend off lust" through various techniques of "wholesome Christian communication": men should pray only with men, and women with women. Counseling should also be gender-confined, they said, as it is dangerous for men to be with women when they are in a "vulnerable state." In the highly unlikely event that a man had no choice but to counsel a woman, he was to keep his office door cracked and make sure a staff member or his wife was nearby for accountability purposes.

And how can we forget the tutorials about physical contact. Let's look at hugging, for example. "Generally, avoid hugging," they told us, "but if you feel you must hug someone, do so by employing *safe hugging practices*." I'll elaborate. I was truly in a meeting where the following were demonstrated.

First, the side hug:

Position yourself to the side of the person you will be hugging. Place an arm around the back of the person, and then gently squeeze the opposite shoulder. Be sure to keep the contact brief.

Next, the A-hug:

The two huggers lean toward each other, their heads forming the apex of the letter "A." Each person's arms reach around the other's shoulders and back to create the horizontal line in the letter. The two bodies bend at the waist and strain forward — avoiding contact at all costs — to form the diagonal lines.

It is my conviction that hugging techniques and office doors left half-open during counseling sessions are not the best weapons in heaven's arsenal against lust and sexual misconduct. As we discussed in chapters 1 and 2, the root of sin is within. If the root of inappropriate thoughts and feelings toward women is not dealt with, all the safety measures we employ can be in vain. A wide-open office door and one's wife being in the very next room will not restrain the imagination of a man who has lust in his heart. While merely shaking the hand of a woman, he may be entertaining impure thoughts about her — in which case, so much for the side hug or A-hug protocol.

Personally, I respect others' traditions. I understand the preventative nature of what I call "defensive hugging," but I propose that we reevaluate such measures. I firmly believe that when a sister in Christ gives me a real hug, she demonstrates trust. The fact that she trusts me as a brother elicits respect and honor, facilitating a much safer environment for us to interact in than an environment of fear-based caution or suspicion.

Let's look at my proposal from a different angle. Was side hugging a necessary precaution in the upper room of Acts 1, where Jesus' followers—men and women both—awaited the Holy Spirit? I do not believe that was the case. That room was filled with Christian camaraderie and honor. Everyone had paid a price to follow Christ and to be present in that gathering. Moreover, the group was keenly focused on the assignment Jesus had given. In a room like that, sin had no power. The stakes were high and love was pure.

As a body of believers who are passionately pursuing God and His ways, we have been privileged at times to experience a certain tipping point in the room, a state in which His presence and glory fully satisfy us and there is no room for any sin to raise its head in our midst.

Moments, and sometimes seasons, like these usher in an effortless, magnificent level of purity and honor. Sin is unthinkable, and if while looking within we find any unwholesome thoughts or issues, we deal with them immediately and effectively. We realize that what we have stepped into is too precious, that our opportunity to participate in transforming people, regions, and nations is too great to jeopardize with carnality. In short, there *is* a place where sin can't touch us—a state of being where purity triumphs and God's power flows through us.

The body of Christ has assumed a defensive posture about most matters pertaining to sexuality and the relationships between men and women. Our general mindset is that we live in a fallen world, we are prone to lust, and we should take all necessary precautions so that we do not fail. Thus, we have focused most of our energies on playing defense. Have we considered the alternative? Have we explored the possibilities of an offense strategy?

Consider this example: Jesus said, "Whoever looks at a woman to lust for her has already committed adultery with her in his heart" (Matthew 5:28). How have Christians always interpreted this verse? "If you think it, you've done it." Out of a fear of "thinking it" while in close proximity to women—anywhere in our daily lives, from offices to prayer gatherings—men have deemed it best to avoid interactions with women or to establish awkward, stringent rules to govern them (women pray only for women, men for men).

Why have we not been encouraged to consider the other half of the story, the part that was not directly stated by Jesus but is still very much present in what He said? If our evil thoughts can render us guilty of sin, as if we had actually committed the act, wouldn't pure, upright, and wholesome thoughts have the exact opposite effect? If we can think and imagine ourselves doing evil, thus becoming guilty of evil, couldn't we also use our imaginations to release good? Absolutely!

In the last chapter we examined the purity in Boaz, which made him unafraid of having a woman next to him. There was not even a hint that Boaz did not trust himself or Ruth, not a hint of concern about what could happen in the night, in the dark, away from eyes and other people. There was a purity in Boaz that made him secure enough to ask Ruth to stay by him until morning. Boaz was not playing defense.

Why do we live in fear? Fear does not protect us. Purity protects us. To the pure, all things are pure. So, if I hug someone as my sister, lust is going to be the last thing on my mind, because we have this amazing relationship as brother and sister in Christ and we are building God's Kingdom together. Why would I forfeit such privilege?

While some church cultures continually remind us how lustful and dirty we are, we must supersede that idea by demonstrating relationships that are pure, that set an example to the world, and that make onlookers say, "I admire the way they interact."

(Danielle)

Marios and I had not been to a meeting outside our denomination for 11 years when the prophetic intercession group invited us, and we were curious. I will never forget the love and freedom we experienced in that meeting. Worship was fully engaging, with people lying prostrate, visibly touched by the presence of God. The speaker ministered words of tangible love, and then administered an altar call. She explained that her team would be coming out to hug people. They were not going to pray, just hug people. This was the first time we'd been in a service where the "hugging protocol" went out the window. We were a bit nervous, but open. That day would change our lives.

We encountered people with pure hearts, who walked in truth and genuine love for us, though we'd just met. There were no questions regarding our position or platform, and there was honor for men and women alike. As we drove away, we agreed that although we didn't understand all that happened in the meeting, Love and purity were there, and it was worth everything.

This encounter with Love cast out all fear, and we were going after exactly that—God's pure love, no turning back. In the days that followed, we sought Yahweh with all of our hearts, and discovered that as we fell in love with Him, the relationships we were building reflected the same kind of substance. They were honest, sometimes difficult, but ultimately fruitful.

Since those days when we decided to passionately pursue Yahweh, we have chosen to establish relationship and community with those who are brave enough to be vulnerable, honest, and trustworthy. Consequently, the environment of our home and church community is one that is fueled by unconditional love and empowerment, where life flourishes.

(Marios)

Danielle and I have been walking out this type of life-flourishing pursuit, and we now have a place within a body of people where this is our norm. We have experienced the truth and power of purity. We are free to be, and along with our community we have enjoyed many years of peace in the area of relationships. Immorality and infidelity have no place in our midst.

Both of us have individual relationships that we cultivate with people of the opposite gender all over the world, and we have no issues with that. Why? Because we are pure. Being in right relationship, in an atmosphere of true purity, releases the power to be who we were called to be. It helps us establish the strategic relationships that God needs to accomplish his purposes and to increase his government without end.

(Danielle)

We continue to be on the greatest adventure of our lives, walking toward the fullness of Ish and

Ishshah, in the image of our Creator. Weeds pop up here and there, but we recognize them and are not afraid. By trusting in the love and life of Yahweh, every step of the way, we are confident He is directing our path. Pure and powerful, we choose to journey on!

EPILOGUE

A few seconds had elapsed since the chairman of the credentialing committee had posed his question. The candidate shot one quick glance into each set of eyes that bore down on him. He wanted to acknowledge them, but also to communicate that he was by no means intimidated by their stern looks. The evil that the committee, and the entire movement, was so preoccupied with had no hold on the candidate. He had nothing to hide, nothing to fear. The candidate directed his gaze on the chairman, breathed in slowly, and smiled. His face radiated confidence, and his voice conveyed clarity of thought and authority. He was not merely answering the question; he was establishing his posture for the rest of the interview. He was taking his stand for the duration of his time with the organization. He desired what they desired – purity and uprightness – but not out of fear. Out of love. Perfect love. The Father's love. The love that protects and forgives and empowers God's Sons.

"No, absolutely not!" he replied.

Sexual purity, decency, and a general moral and ethical uprightness cannot be attained simply because we try hard and wish to avoid the painful consequences of failure in such areas. A wholesome life stems from a wholesome perspective. As in the case of healthy plants and trees, whatever grows above ground is the product of a healthy root system beneath. We act based on who we are inside; and who we are depends in large part on our worldview and beliefs. I believe Yahweh's love is the most significant catalyst available to mankind for healthy lives and relationships. God's own Son, Jesus Christ, willingly came to our world, lived a sinless life, and demonstrated love to the utmost — even laying down His life to make a way for love to win. Christ's sacrifice — God's ultimate gift of love to us — gives Man and Woman, Ish and Ishshah, a winning chance to eradicate erroneous mindsets and to reform bad behaviors. To return to First Estate, shamelessly walking in intimacy with God and one another.

Danielle and I shared what we have been learning on our journey, fully believing that the love we have as individuals and as a couple will make a difference. Fully believing that every Ish and Ishshah around the world will rise to the fullest of their potential, to properly steward what God has given us, together.

36616574R00063

Made in the USA
Columbia, SC
04 December 2018